T0166589

VULGAR MECHANICS

VULGAR MECHANICS

K. B. THORS

Coach House Books | Toronto

first edition

Published with the generous assistance of the Canada Council for the Arts and the Ontario Arts Council. Coach House Books also acknowledges the support of the Government of Canada through the Canada Book Fund and the Government of Ontario through the Ontario Book Publishing Tax Credit.

LIBRARY AND ARCHIVES CANADA CATALOGUING IN PUBLICATION

Title: Vulgar mechanics / K. B. Thors.
Names: Billey, K. T., 1987- author.
Description: Poems.
Identifiers: Canadiana (print) 20190141204 | Canadiana (ebook) 20190141298 | ISBN 9781552453988 (softcover) | ISBN 9781770566194 (PDF) | ISBN 9781770566187 (EPUB)
Classification: LCC PS8603.I435 V85 2019 | DDC C811/.6—DC23

Vulgar Mechanics is available as an ebook: ISBN 978 1 77056 918 7 (EPUB); ISBN 978 1 77056 619 4 (PDF)

Purchase of the print version of this book entitles you to a free digital copy. To claim your ebook of this title, please email sales@chbooks.com with proof of purchase. (Coach House Books reserves the right to terminate the free digital download offer at any time.

TABLE OF CONTENTS

III

For Mona, Nyja, and Layla

'the fuel of our oppression
is the fuel of freedom too
oooo oooo oooo'

– k. d. lang, 'Acquiesce,'
All You Can Eat

'I arise in the morning torn between a
desire to improve the world and a desire
to enjoy the world. This makes it hard to
plan the day.'

– E. B. White

GIRL GIVES BIRTH TO THUNDER

It was more a clearing
of space than conception, a slice

less electric than imagined.
Lightning rods are crosshairs

of least resistance, so why
go out of your way

to carve cold-room
root cellars for another

collapsed shaft
of parenthood? The wedge we

want is a clamour – cutline
access to seismic legacy data.

Earthquakes are new around
here, diamond-tip drilled.

A grand idea: falling in love
with a quarter section, then spelling

sky out for the rest of my life.
Riding this derrick all the way

down until someone drowns or
drops a match and it all goes up

and on again, down the road
to a reserve town

where the tap water isn't
yet flammable.

There's no such thing as legal land
description in the province

of weather modification – home
of eugenics and clouds scalloped

with silver iodine. They say it
prevents hail from ruining crops.

Somewhere between hoodoos
riddled with spit cups I ripped this spare

pair of truck balls from the winch,
packing my lip with lift-kit

stomping grounds, this
generation hand to mouth.

Count the mountains
between contractions – let's

get ready to rumble. Baiting
the prairie is disaster – synapse

gone lickety-split
to seed, rigging

my itch to piledrive
a personal well.

If I could frack
this spine

I would.

Fuck derring.
We epidural-do.

THE LONG-FINGERED DRAW

How satisfying, the snip
through spring sod.

Did you imagine construction
paper children? Dried reeds
by the river?

I want that instrument
to be my home.

I want to hear the storm
crack and suppose

tectonic swell when
the table gives out

under me and you
hold eye contact.

Take three trains.

Come over and tell me
I don't need brass knuckles
to kill this clover.

Tell me in creeks.

YOUR STOMACH OR MINE?

The sun is thin, the air is triage, and you,
you're an acolyte – an adult falcon

gutcheck: where the screech came from.
Goes. Feeds. It's no injury, no

sand on new graves or one-night bout
of grief. When the power cut out

I called twice, afraid to forget how
onslaught behaves: lighting red

votives, brunching by the robin's-egg
church. Ask me how bruises change

colour as you supervise this hack job
through your last cross-stitch.

Spin my funeral necklace just so
it hides the vulgar mechanics, the hook

and eye of death turning tricks.
I heard it. It left a message in

metallic thread on the mirror
that broke in the squall, so I let

my molars rot and made batteries
with the fillings. Tin foil

feels better, biting down.
There's a little bit of enemy

in everyone I love, and this
is updraft, beat by beat, and tailspin.

Nothing umbilical about it.

WHAT'S LOVE GOT TO DO WITH IT

Except as the engine
of absence, lace

puddling below
the window.

Eulogy: an edgewise
word. What's the point

of freedom
of speech

if I'm not open
to conversation?

The question I
pose is a lunge

I can stack
as long as I want
as loud as I want.

There's a name for it.

To stick to my guns and
kiss who she couldn't.

There's a phrase that fits:
I don't believe in either-or

but in hindsight
she could have been.

ORAL HEALTH

Of course I flossed her corpse. Before it was cold.
Before it was a corpse.

CLUTCHES, STRUTS, AND BRAKES (I)

I. Clutches

Enable transmission
from one component
to another, whenever

power or motion must
be controlled in amount
or over time.

II. Struts

The reduction
of unsprung

weight improves
handling, and ride.

III. And Brakes

It is normal
for them to be
mounted rigidly

with respect
to the body
of the vehicle.

SELF-PORTRAIT: SKULL AND ORNAMENT

after Méret Oppenheim

No sooner had Flood found her bracelet
than they chopped off her hand. Standard
punishment for counting cards, she replied
with an abacus of pearls. Baba's freshwaters
became a pain scale proving trauma can tally

if not sync. The X-ray is my maternal self, piqued
interest in women – the deluge concept, dommeing
what she didn't get around to. So what if earrings
compromise the scan? Bangles are shifty and even
before, her wrists were rattling axles. If you had

one body for the rest of your life, how
would you top it? What's one bridge you want
to burn before the water reaches our chins?
My answer to most things is Flood – fur
on the saucer, dirt-filtered tea. I can't build a boat

but I can face my face and when the clouds burn
off I'll sprawl just outside her field of vision. She
a femur distilled by the sun, me a bleached-out familiar
faking a shrug. *Stick around this time. See what happens.*
But there's noise below the image, her captioned lip reads *No
Higher Resolution Available.* Miles from the cemetery, I consider

that an epitaph. The four of us, pacing the prairie. Her C-sections, her stage four. I inherited this arm hair – the switch that trips when an ant crawls up my sleeve. Call this a statement piece, set in stone. A decent hand tossed on the table. Four of a kind passing the shovel. Peacock bouquet in a heat always hybrid.

CAKE

If I shave the moustaches of famous dictators
into my pubic hair, do I cease to be a threat?

When I detonate my body I become
an embrace but the issue remains –

what does it mean to be taken seriously
when the perfect woman is an antique

trumpet: an instrument that will
ruin your lips.

SELF-PORTRAIT AS SULPHUR

As in, that which occurs often,　　in seams
narrowed by revelry　　　　　　and war.

Calm never comes that comes　　to all
but even if I were the wine　　　of wrath, rising steady
　　　　　　　　　　　　　　as steam
　　　　　　　　　　　　　　　　along the highway,

that's relatively clean heat　　　　　for every house.

Powder for each cheek　　　　　　of hallowed ground,
papier mâché　　　　　　　　　　and marbled girl.

Call me hot stuff.
Spin spider silk hoods　　　　　so you see
　　　　　　　　　　　　　not light but edible
　　　　　　　　　　　　　darkness – the ship above
　　　　　　　　　　　　　　　the last white whale.

Sublimate mammals　　　　　into manageable form
and the name　　　　　　　　flowers. *Is* flower.

Call me brimstone.

Sing my lungs and bathe　　　the letters
the lashes that spell　　　　　the brightest salt.

WHAT'S WITH THE GIRLS?

Between the Wig Boutique and the last round
of radiation, Mom knew something was wrong
with my sisters and me. *Out with it.* The night before,
while our aunt stayed in the hospital with Mom,
that uncle went into my little sister's bedroom
asking for a hug and muttering about virginity.

She got away, shaking in my basement room where
our voices woke our older sister. She'd warned us
about him – he'd cornered her when she was a teenager
years prior – I'd been on guard since thirteen. Back then,
Mom's response was that he'd tried the same on her.
There was a meeting at which he agreed to get counselling
and they decided not to tell the cousins, his children, the family.

That morning at the Cross Cancer Institute, a different story
spilled out. He didn't try the same thing with my mom, he serially raped
her for years. As a teen she'd gone to live with her sister to escape
a violent father. On her deathbed she wasn't angry, she was heartbroken
that her sister, my aunt, couldn't admit that she had known.
Not that she didn't or couldn't do anything.
He'd go from her bed to mine.

Confronted by our cousins, he didn't deny it. He'd been in love
with two women, he said. His wife and her middle-school-aged sister.

Mom's final weeks were spent unloading. On the farm, girls talked about molestation on the way to school, it was unnamed normal.

For her it started at nine, her older brother's friends. That brother hadn't believed her but at her burial the one surviving 'family friend' she named didn't deny anything either.

He did, standing beside the church after lunch in the hall, tell me he didn't *see why this is coming up now.*

COMME DES GARÇONS

For my eighteenth birthday my parents gave me a yellow plastic whistle
and a *Roads of Alberta* book of maps. Walking home with headphones
in bare legs in the dark, how often I've done such stupid things. Day look
at night, no keys spiked between my fingers, a vulnerable population

walking fast because it feels good and velocity involves direction – better
seem like you know where you're going when scared. This means of
admitting that I am scared, often. That the world is not for me
to walk through. Music is key to these stretches. Prince cuts through

clumps of college boys, Frank Ocean Bed-Stuy, the train a bridge above
my rattling teeth. Not for the first time I think if someone were raped
tonight, better me than them. Quotas in the age of Turing laws,
posthumous pardons. Why not take one for the team?

The Black man drops his shoulders as he rounds the corner,
assuming my fear as we smile, each trying to disarm the other. I'd bawl
if I weren't so spoiled but I'm imagining myself in the hospital, cloying
Amélie revamping the scene. I'd wear that paper gown, it wouldn't

wear me. They don't know who they got, I'd think. No victory in them
not getting anything – more mass for the black hole, the heart with two
eyes. Last spring I bought a whistle in a vintage shop on International
Women's Day. Tonight I skipped a poetry reading to stay in, write this

and learn ASL for green, yellow, red. The Supreme Court has no safe word,
might as well play in traffic. My whistle's brass now. We came to
terms with the distaff race, called a few shots. It's masc4masc I'm after
tonight, sipping boyish croon. They sell distressed yet relaxed style

and agendered perfume by the Flatiron building. I've never starched
a shirt, not sure I'd press charges. Restorative justice assumes a starting
point and French had last century. What's next? What does it mean
to Pop Life? Rape Culture is an imperative form. Ready to wear.

AND RESPONSE

Sensing ourselves
prey in that predicament,

we sought shelter
in an ox carcass,

scraping its walls
for strings of protein.

We did it for warmth,
we said, over handfuls

of cat's cradle.
And sure, it's fucking cold

in the ribs, but there never
was a shortage of heat.

We just needed a reason
to rub our palms,

someone to sniff the needles
after we pissed in the pines,

whistling while we worked.
We were children then,

pre-war and soft-core,
cracking the code

of our shiny one-piece.
That warping favourite.

SMOKE SIGNAL

Call me when your hair decides to curl and chase
my eyes around the fire. I'll be squatting by the river, peeling

poplar saplings. Didn't you say that bruise
went yellow then purple – a berry full of spiders, destined

for pie? When you disappeared behind the bend
we don't name, I fed my stack of switches

to first-person flames, listening to sap crack
into lighter fluid. Licks of bark burn too. All I can

spare is a stir stick, something to rough up the coals
before I tie on a tarp to snap at the clouds. But no matter

how hard the backdraft, how hyperextended

my neck, this muleta taunts only myself. I'm no matador
but I can call bullshit, stuffing my face with saskatoons.

I need to make the most of what I can't help
hacking down, so I aim the bellows of this

white flag your way. When the wind comes
I want you to see me, loud and clear.

ATLANTIC CROSSING

You thought I lacked facility
for foreign language, but there are depths
of mastery, my darling,

my hedged bet. It's no one's fault
you heard *harder* when I said *during*.

Don't worry, epidermis, I said,
over and softly again.

You are my emergency
contact, scratched out twice

until you admit this
ink is an anchor, shifting
at my mention of wing.

You want a challenge, something
unearthly. How do I say

I have legs for that? What are the words
for *consider our phases* –

Jupiter in storm, Io as stitch on the tongue.

There is no having. There is only the tide.
One eye open, and then the other.

MISSIVE FROM A FORMER MASTODON

In the future   people   love each other
and their legs   look like ours   hollering across the yard.

More than aggression   in the goose pen   hair
and glands   this is a watershed   a Flood, because

the second you see   yourself   as bigger than
                       anything   else, you begin

to decompose   a sibling
witnessing   a softening.

A species   of limestone clock   layer of gravel.
A spiral   laughing at its own   bad aim.

ON THE QUESTION OF WHO SHE IS

You were bashful and warm, my argument for men
and women being friendly, until the autumn you left
a stare lying around for anatomy to pick up and ply

into proper goodbyes. You taught me to hitchhike
and that I am selfish. You stopped asking important
questions: whether I remember your second-favourite

constellation, that sketchy ride out of Croatia,
the angry border and two wrong trains that took us
to Verona, or your picture of me wearing all grey

in June, blending into the concrete under Juliet's balcony.
Smaller, weaker, I can hold her down and I do
because in all my quiet practices, I never

underestimate the physicality of control.
She has this too-soft cheek I'll someday smash
with kisses and roll in her cigarettes until we cough

our smithereens to a laugh. I want her to come
when I cross the street. If she were hungry I'd build
her a church, and I told her about you. So now I stay

still and wait, on the surface, on the tension of the wet
reflections in my eyes, signs that will certainly be
taken for some sort of currency, held up as evidence

that I push too hard, that nature has laws,
that the beauty of life is that it's impossible
to be sated. To relax. To say that actually, I have

nightmares about scratching records
on the underside of her thigh, and this morning
the dirt under my nails doesn't remind me of you.

CLUTCHES	STRUTS	AND BRAKES (II)
A spool of barb wire	defining a fence	caught
my calf	on the way down	and now
the longest scar	on the body of a woman	you can't consider
	attractive means	
	stretch marks, more-than	over-expressed
	collagen – that is, the birthing	
	glue –	collage as consent.
Clots are provisions		
a set of lips		
	I pack	for the long haul
		of hankering,
my blood let	alone	on the dotted line
a time signature	an autograph	of highway
	in irons	
	saying this	
	is how I hit	
	the road	the spot
		the hay
		the jackpot.

MOJO RISING

What happens to the cunt when the stomach corrodes

through nights spent cramped in fetal position?

It becomes a will, equipped with its own rhetorical questions.

If I bleed this fever all the way out, do I get time

to myself? If I am in fact a lucky little lady

in a city of light, god forbid my mercury

give me away. I can't forbid anything.

I barely regulate my own body

temperature. But what do I know?

I just got into town about an hour ago.

for Jesse

I learn what an Alberta Snowstorm is in a Williamsburg cafe called the West – after Mae, a Brooklynite – hamstring stuck to a pseudo-industrial barstool. High summer in the city, garbage juice gutters. If Felicity is a name, Complicity Porter lives here. Got real into fermenting last year.

'...the men stand in a circle around the woman, who is kneeling on the ground. They circle jerk, ejaculating so she is covered in "snow." They then proceed to gang-bang the woman – pausing to tweak on crystal meth. Originated in Ft. McMurray, Alberta, where due to the oil sands there is a largely transient population of male workers and relatively few females.'

– Urban Dictionary, 2018

The rig pig I knew best was a genius. The male teachers who labelled him a problem kid were my cheerleaders – best for bright girls to steer clear of that kind of boy. Unrescued from boredom he became a troubled teen, a walking DUI who intimidated the calculus teacher then went north to work. We met in town every Christmas, he made my little sister laugh by ordering every possible Starbucks modification, extra whip non-fat sugarless double pump. We discussed the news. Quiznos opened again – during the boom it closed for lack of teen labour. Even on a downturn, there's always money for a guy who can add. Cash for tatts, trucks, drugs, girls. I wonder what else he could have done, how wondering makes me an asshole. When I texted him about the Snowstorm, he replied in redneck meme:

Cologne for gas hands: WD40.

He died of undetermined causes, probably fentanyl. I walk to the train past fresh condo graffitti. Hot pink caps read FUCK MARRY KILL, but vertical.

TO JUPITER AND HIS ORANGE EYE

Craning my neck from your porch swing
I watch the morning glory close her saloon,

right on cue. Would that we were all so consistent,
that we had proper time and place. Something nice

to wink at, off to the side. Observe an expert
introduction to an unbroken horse

before you lay hands on anyone else –
some of us need the peripheral approach,

the fistful of sugar and pressed silver
buckle. When the time comes, I'll fill

your temple with leather working
tools – everything you need to accommodate

the tamer's impulse. Slim autumn fashions.
Lend me your shoulder bulk and monocle

squint, let's read the maelstrom. Massage that crick.
The paper can't crinkle if we never recline.

COLLATERAL:

A backless dress. The closest
I came to the shackle, scapula

in the field, my hilt studding his soil

for a change. Not knowing how
to barter, we stripped the pillory

for parts and built a tower
for red-tailed hawks.

Flight patterns are concentric,
in terms of fuel economy –

biomimicry is a study
in circles: the rim of glass, our fusing

coccyx. Always trying to achieve that
great migration inward, I declare a truce,

a trinity of give and take for us
to talk too much about. We are

pretty tired. I passed out like this, hungry
and halter-topped, hoping

he'd thumb the blade.
Check my leather bomber, his

jean jacket. Nothing in the pocket
but a bent ID.

LADY DRIVEN

lady cop lady liberty lady
macbeth lady like
lady and the tramp lady
in waiting lady luck
lay lady lay lady
parts lady in red but really

The transmission's in good shape
for the mileage. They just don't push as hard.

FORT WORTH (NÉE NORMANDEAU BUT WASKASOO)

When summer's over I'll salvage every string
of white lights and wind them around your clubhouse.

Rough charm among trees, it will be the crinoline
you always wanted, a ring around your Adam's apple.

I'll call this my one and only.
I'll call it fortress.

See, I'm capable of building
codes – look how

decent it is now. Dripping girly
drapery, itching

to make the most of those lines.
Before a white hotel afraid

of rebellion, this was a river
crossing. Seam, seamstress.

See rose riser. Decline
the noun when they curtsey.

Lap up my pearl necklace
before she becomes a moat.

THE HISTORY OF THE UNDERHAND PITCH

I. Researching

how my hands   cracked   that mouth   on her
                                       a raw sun   rising

II. If It's Just a Lob With a Name

where do I direct this dread, if not   the spindrift
                    the 88 stitches   between the first snow
                    and our popped fly

                                           the forest silence
                                           and the last latch   click

III. Or the Future of Sport

I don't know   the width between   our bodies
which I or she this is   on deck, looking to catch
                                              the striped story arc

but the scuff   on our cheek
                         can't quite freeze   and this state of undress

says leave well   enough   alone, but where
                         is enough   and how, when

all I sing for sits   beside me, an olive an ache   to steal third

IV. And Melting

where do I direct this   dread   when my body begs to differ?

DRUNK TANK

The only record of that burlesque was the sonnet
we found on the floor, a trampled sheet we tried to preserve
in simple syrup and steel-toed boots. She started to fester

around happy hour – a minor wound. A new island.
We built her a home with our palsied will to please: glass-ceiling

windshield, boy-short chamois. We couldn't tell
if it was an aggressor or a cabin, car, or display case.

It didn't matter. The louder the saws the later we stayed,
declaring ourselves sociology students, spectators, friends
of the mastiff plastered above the urinal. We appropriated that

Mutt R. meter too, and let people watch the porcelain drop
into our ant farm, settling between diets on the rocks and a skull

full of castles. Pro tip: to piss standing up, bear down
while jutting out. Turbidity is proof of life in a lake –
I packed my fire poke cum stir stick for a couple reasons.

I'm trying to make a pass at self-fulfilled prophecy, to fancy
myself an active ingredient, the chain you pull to drench the catwalk.
Pangaea wasn't a meeting of the minds, she was thirsty

work. The charge is past perfect – *disorderly* don't mean
squat. The lipstick on my cheek is intentional. It's called lava.

KITCHEN SCRAP

There have been inventions
since last month. Colours,

salt craving, meat
wrapped in comics. Empty

trees receive their tenants
and he can't stop

sleeping, in this heat, my syphon
hand. I can't decide.

Do I become small again,
a little boy blue?

Gild toy horses
with elephant paint

and trespass
again, against him?

REVERSE COWGIRL

I can't promise not to laugh but yes, sir,
I'll jump your gun. I'll ride that handlebar
all the livelong day, all the way home

crying *wolf* and *foul* and *love me*
tender. As long as the holster's real –

soft enough to warrant such fuss,
hard enough to crack. A tool belt

slung on a fresh hand,
dealer's choice: the deep end
for this flop, turn, and river.

Of course you cut the cards.
You think I could stack the deck
against you? Oh babe.

Ante up.

Don't let me get away with this.
Playing dumb, and winning.

MINERAL BLOCK

You already regret the dragonfly. The larvae
it won't eat, the itch that threads our fingers.
Show me the underbelly, the trough, lymph

spread into mortar, and don't be surprised
if I grovel at your grave. Don't be afraid when
I kiss your neck with the heel of my hand.

Next time you take your love out
on something so small, let me know
after the fact. Let a little blood from my face first.
Leave me a corner to lick through the winter.

I left my nipple clamps at the Chrysler factory
in Windsor. They felt at home on the assembly
line where my host turns into a machine eight hours a day
wearing gloves that slide into my DMs, forensic-
like. She performs the same act the entire shift –
as honest as a person can be without leaving
fingerprints. It wasn't the factory so much
as her kitchen counter, chain slithering around
our empty case of OV. What can you expect
from a toy with fixed teeth yet adjustable jaws –
still life with Kirkland drum of coconut oil and
beef jerky, bottle cap mise en place. The next
morning a bartender named Rose tells other
customers *this is a no-straw establishment*
then slides a paper-wrapped tube toward my
Caesar. The factory came later, where the straight
girls – *the* she says, the straight girls ask how
two women even have sex. Even have, her arms paw
printed. She knows all about their vaginas, the Pap
smears their boyfriends don't have time for. I want
her to tell them they can leave marks so blue. That
I squirted all over the laminate, a Skene gland gone
wild beside her extra deep sink, a pool of fluid
seeping under the fridge. I want to say I squirted once
in high school while watching *A Beautiful Mind* –
because it was long, I like to think – and not again

til twenty-eight and on the rebound. The James Dean of Detroit
Lesbians doesn't fret about her fascination with
crime. She DMs me pictures of guns and when
we say she gets something it's hard, not wet.
What's the over–under Rose was aiming at
our omelettes – the other set of clamps.

EXORSISTER

she taught me to read with the Billy Goats Gruff
and I reported her missing two days ago

the big one tosses trolls over the bridge
so smaller ones can eat sweet grass

there's no safe distance in a, from a
psych ward. The world is one
big underlying condition:

personality	disorder	post-pussy grab
symptomatic	aggravated	assault
survivor	guilt	sounded out

Nobody can reject an organ on another girl's behalf.

TANK TOP

If Flood were an animal she would
be a woman, a pressed pair of slacks
otherwise known as centuries

of calves, sliding over each other
earthwise. A conveyor belt
getting us around. Aggressive

tread provides traction on soft terrain
but damages paved surfaces, so choose
your own adventure. Ride-on or rodeo.

Cobblestones, or both. It's a trick question
of course, an ode to role reversals –
I love a good shirt sleeve

but bare is better for the dance floor
where we take charge of this topsy-turvy
temporary outfit: power

steering, my armoured vehicle
pad-mounted transformer.
Sometimes the bottom high-centres

and the shift in voltage brews
what we might call modern weather:
bulldozer vision and wider wide opens.

The tide is a thrall rising up
on hind legs so the best we can hope
for is a tongue lying flat, a watershed

at the back of my throat
saying ah ah ah –
après nous le déluge.

RESTING BITCH FACE DAUGHTER OF THOR

'Did anyone ever tell you you're angry when you're beautiful?'
                          – Q to Captain Kathryn Janeway

In 1906 an ox was slaughtered at a country fair.
Francis Galton observed a contest to guess its weight –
the average more accurate than most individuals, a tendency
to truth called *wisdom of the crowd*. Galton was knighted
for statistics, a laundry list. A century later, four or five
men follow me off the train, bidding into the sunset.
*85. 125. 110, give or take. Girl, you deaf? How much
to break that pelvis?* Bodies at rest will stay at rest.
Bodies in motion will pussyfoot several extra blocks
to go anywhere other than home. Galton also coined
nature versus nurture. A jaw set to deter, a stride
calibrated to get away without seeming to hurry, a lack
of reaction suggesting you don't hear but wouldn't dare
ignore them. Male, terf, navel – a gaze is a gaze is a.
In Romance languages packed with pink tax my name
sounds like face, darling, the feminine form of expensive.
In Icelandic the word for sheep is kind, as in one of a
group that would snap my Rorschach hips. *Share
the wishbone.* Those guys did zero in on my weight
but birds have fused clavicles to withstand
the rigours of flight. The crux of wisdom of the crowd is
the collective must be *diverse and independently deciding*.
Borg means city so resistance is a heel, a slew of sprained
ankles climbing back into the ring after each foiled misery

scene. Mjölnir, my ready-to-hand wormhole. What if everyone had hammers on their garters while walking the street? A variety of tongues in the tongue-in-cheek, declaring ourselves and all our pre-existing conditions worth a lick. A wink of salt in the quantum salad.

My sister helps my dad rip up planks from the deck,
a ship of Theseus under bacon fat for birds. A question of identity.

I used to care about that kind of thing.
Now I care about not getting shot.
About my brother not getting shot.
About his boyfriend not going to jail
when someone yells *Fag* across the street.

There are refugees beside you right now there are people who know
you won't bag their blood when they're bleeding out.
Guys at home say they hope a gay bar does
open downtown – easy to get a bat, shoot
fish in a barrel.

A sash full of powder strapped to your body,
bachelorette bedsore, caking the hull.
When ship becomes casket we gather at the shore
and burn that sucker down in bulletproof tea gowns.
Skin-tight leopard print, shrunk in the wash.

BINARY POEM

I am	sun	dog
	whip	lash
	own	risk
She is	hatch	back
	low	tech
	bar	bell
We are	neck	and neck
	blunt	force
	blind	fold
	loyalty	program
	trend	forecasting
	riding	the pine
What	hurry	up offence
	good	grief
	portion	control
	honour	system
	resistance	training
After	thigh	gap
	margin	of error
	sickle	cell
	stockholm	syndrome

hereditary	trait
reasonable	doubt
rooting	hormone
beaver	fever

A structurally   sound
   cervical   spine
   plays   red
   rover   red
   rover   obsolete
                   go
                   fish

SOFT PALATE

Say there were buckets.

Scar tissue, tapped at the trunk for years then sloshed
over the brim of the gully.

There's no expansion if the plates don't drift, no two
ways to arrive at this shin-splint overpass of one's own.

Teeth keep our mouths from caving in
while rye in the hip toasts a contrary buttress.

The body suffers no false progress.

Eventually you cross yourself
and your bite will never be the same.

CHAMPAGNE PROBLEMS

Twenty-first-century chivalry: hers and hers single dose
yeast infection treatments, capsules chased with pints
on Jasper Ave. One preventative, a morning after
pill I supply, myself symptomatic on arrival.

Life is like women's hockey: the higher you go
the gayer it gets, but we bicker over words
and her sticks stay under the bed. Tape-wrapped
grips are bacteria traps. Who isn't?

Every job is easier with the right tools but you
know necessity. More than mother-of, she's
the charge in the air our kite collects. I went
to Shoppers for Canesten, not condoms. To redefine

bottleneck: wipe down the mouth, make sure
the label is smooth or removed, hydrate, and look
out for chemistry. Sugar does a number
on cunt pH – the only real pissing contest

is with yourself. The world is our limit
the sky is our oyster – let's not rule that wine
cellar–Oiler cage out. Cheers, to the combo
pack of jumbo condiments. An impulse purchase.

NATURE CHANNEL

When the scare owl ceases to be effective, pick it up
and throw it at the pigeons. Choreograph snowplows
to exfoliate freeways or jackknife a semi to dam up
some tow trucks. Trust me. The cattle will adapt.

WINNING THE THREE-LEGGED RACE

Your pulse confronts
my fingers, the ones I used
to scale frozen waterfalls

in deep winter, spines
of wax dripping down
this taper. Knuckles find

doubt in your sternum
and a certain light, freedom –
oil on one side,

air on the other –
the perfect coupling
a hinge needs to swivel.

If you make it to the cathedral
shed, everything will improve.
You will be a sliver in the crease

of a larger finger and I will love
you in our fine unrest – until we forget
which coffin runs on kerosene

or because everything with joints
can kneel and does. At least once
before morning, when we lurch to

the finish line and picnic where
the wick sputters. Where lichen
limbs topple swayback barns.

VELOCITY RAPTURE

for Sando and Gord

The Creation Science Museum has vinyl siding and a pterodactyl
etched into a headstone on the front lawn. Around the corner

my brother and I are staging the best Big Valley Jamboree
psychobilly ever saw, Dayne Age meets Jurassica Lange, 3D

anniversary edition. We snatch their tea-stained parchment
tracing British royals to Eden and read it to Michael's scrapbook
filth because Belle's library is always open and fundamentalism

is a pussy on fire. The church sign in Olds says *tragically hic
welcome*: a tip we stash with the trilobites they use to prove the Flood.

They say the Ark's prow is around here somewhere, the drag equivalent
of drag equivalent – Ann Adam Aunt Eve serving how the west was

won the house down. When Kipling said hell he meant hunger
game in glaciated hills, a leaked J-Law of motion. Every time the radio
says, *see my sister got raped so a man got killed,* I feel somewhat

safer. Same pattern on the table same clock on my lace-front
cunt. The next queen's name is Consequence: a rising star.

She throws clay on my wheel and pumps the pedal to announce
her sister Consuela, Consolation, a Latinx dually recasting crew

cut, how we lip sync for our lives every time a man tells us to
have a blessed day / smile, beautiful / sculpt another mug squat. Not all
but ally. Some men walk first through waist-deep snow and fashion

pillowcase slings for our broken arms. Some plains are holographic
Canadian tuxedos, a purple martin in a top hat, trying his best. How
do we improve – the oil field paid Rapture to take dignitaries to gas wells,
where she'd torch their saddles long enough to cure hearts so hard

they shred like parm. The place that happens is weltschmerz tar,
reclaimed barnwood, and buckskin femme. A masc sequence gown
in a new era of set design. Holding the stool, finding the stud.

ALTER EGO

À la seam ripper cum scythe – string
theory plucked out stitch by step.
Pants become a smock real
fast when serge pulls loose from the ankle
up, a sine wave sea serpent above and
below the surface. Prodigal gender
survey says: science is a death rattle
and love is to be humbled by nature
so I want to bend over boyfriend
for all the right reasons. Why not
hew his ribs from my spine with an exit
axe and swing them behind my back
like doors on a Lambo? Our lungs scissor
as they hot-air-balloon skyward.
A constant shimmer of the line, or
instead. The snake eating tail is
a magic eye, a mouth always
open, unhinging jaw. The project
now is a glacier in a grain of sand.
Keeping myself scarce, full
of dissolve and about to enjoy
a bigger changeling bang. I mean
oh make me over –
I'm all
I'm gonna be.

CLUTCHES, STRUTS, AND BRAKES (III)

I finally coughed up the triptych
in the back of my throat.

The wrench, the storm,
the centaur waist –

the suspense with which
I hold my own.

ALL THE RAGE

Looking down at ourselves
the way we look at a dropped orange
speaks to the need for a singular

moon. A one-of world to leave
us wanting fistfuls of geodes.
Landscapes.

What they're moulting remains
to be seen. What can be said
for certain: the future will admit

the heart is that which digs
in the deserted village.

The thunder egg
bucking the fire pit.

Kick a rock from the edge
and an echo will say
it takes just as many legs

to unhinge yourself
as there are constellations
in our blind spots.

'Girl Gives Birth To Thunder': Track 1 on *Jock Jams, Volume 1* is Michael Buffer's 'Let's Get Ready to Rumble.' Fiona Apple's 'To Your Love' taught me the phrase 'derring-do.'

'What's Love Got To Do With It' is clearly indebted to Tina Turner.

'Clutches, Struts, and Brakes (1)' is found text from Wikipedia articles on mechanics.

'Self-Portrait: Skull and Ornament' is after Méret Oppenheim's *Self-Portrait, Skull and Ornament, 1964*, also known as 'X-Ray of the Skull of M. O.'

'Self-Portrait as Sulphur' reacts a bit to wine/wrath from Book 1 of Milton's *Paradise Lost*, and fire-and-brimstone traditions at large.

'What's With the Girls?': I've been told that the uncle in this poem was abused when he was ten years old.

'Comme des Garçons' refers to Prince's 'Pop Life.'

'Mojo Rising' took a title and sound bites from The Doors' 'L.A. Woman.'

'Collateral:' riffs on 'I woke up like this' from Beyoncé's song 'Flawless' featuring Chimamanda Ngozi Adichie.

'Kitchen Scrap' uses a line from an 1858 Emily Dickinson letter where she writes that 'The trees receive their tenants.'

'Tank Top': The phrase 'aprés nous le déluge' is attributed to Madame de Pompadour, official chief mistress of Louis xv from 1745 to 1751. The expression came after the Battle of Rossbach, a turning point in the Seven Years War. Critiques of Pompadour, an influential member of the French court and powerful woman not born into aristocracy, were underpinned by anxieties about the breakdown of gender and class hierarchies. The Pompadour hairstyle is named after her. In Dostoyevsky's *The Brothers Karamazov*, 'après nous le déluge' appears as a lamentation of the erosion of Russian values.

'Resting Bitch Face Daughter of Thor': It is convenient that Heidegger uses a hammer as an example of equipment that phenomenologically disappears when in use.

'Velocity Rapture': 'See my sister got raped so a man got killed' and 'Same pattern on the table, same clock...' are from the Tragically Hip song '38 Years Old.' Places happening in the poem refer to the band's song 'Looking for a Place to Happen.'

Re: Hell. In 1907 Rudyard Kipling trekked across Canada and wrote, among other things, 'This part of the country seems to have all hell for a basement, and the only trap door appears to be in Medicine Hat.' He was referring to natural gas deposits. A Big Sugar song and a brewery came later.

'Alter Ego' might be an ode to Hole's *Celebrity Skin*. The blood eagle is an execution style described in skaldic poetry. The subject is brought to kneel and the ribs are cut from the backbone and pried open so the lungs can be lifted out of the body like a pair of wings. In both instances mentioned in the Icelandic Sagas, the blood eagle is done as punishment for patricide. There is ongoing debate as to whether this means of execution is a literary invention, a matter of translation, or actually performed.

ACKNOWLEDGEMENTS

Thank you to the editors of the following publications for including poems from this book: *Arc*, *The Boiler*, *Cake* (UK), *Cosmonauts Avenue*, *CutBank*, *Denver Quarterly*, *filling Station*, *Ghost Proposal*, *Lambda Literary Poetry Spotlight*, *The New Orleans Review*, *Poor Claudia*, *Powder Keg*, *Prelude*, *Room*, *The Rusty Toque*, *Sidekick*, *Vallum*, and *Vinyl*. Thank you also to *Vallum* for awarding their 2015 poetry prize to 'Girl Gives Birth To Thunder' and *Arc* for naming 'Self-Portrait: Skull and Ornament' a 2016 Poem of the Year finalist. The Girls Write Now 2015 anthology includes 'Collateral:'. Composer Rebecca Erin Smith set 'The Long-Fingered Draw' to music and directed its performance at the Manhattan School of Music in April 2016.

I'm grateful to Chris Schafenacker and Bert Almon for helping me realize that poetry is written by living people. Cate Marvin, Lucie Brock-Broido – the Mustang Sally of Examples – Lynn Melnick, and Damian Rogers, for her editorial focus. To my family, for teaching me about care, and Coach House Books.

To the people who lit up the years of these poems, in particular, Amy Macdonald, Rachel Uniat, Jonathan Reich, Carl Severson, Eloísa Díaz, Başak Ulubilgen, Christiaan van Bremen, Sara Nics, Megan Ferrara, John Arthur Greene, Stephen Baidacoff, Jill Swainson, Mike Lombardo, Wendy Mah, and Reg and Wanita Shandro. Mike, H., and that beach beyond words – thank you.

To everyone not believed, with no one to tell, working to break these cycles – you have my utmost.

k. b. thors is a poet, translator, and educator from rural Alberta, Canada. Her translation of *Stormwarning* by Icelandic poet Kristín Svava Tómasdóttir won the American Scandinavian Foundation's Leif and Inger Sjöberg Prize and was nominated for the PEN Literary Award for Poetry in Translation. She is also the Spanish-English translator of *Chintungo: The Story of Someone Else* by Soledad Marambio. Her poems, essays, and literary criticism have appeared around the U.S., U.K., and Canada. She has an MFA from Columbia University, where she was a Teaching Fellow in Poetry. She divides her time between Alberta, Brooklyn, and Montreal.

Typeset in Arno and Gibson

Printed at the Coach House on bpNichol Lane in Toronto, Ontario, on Zephyr
Antique Laid paper, which was manufactured, acid-free, in Saint-Jérôme, Quebec,
from second-growth forests. This book was printed with vegetable-based ink on a
1973 Heidelberg KORD offset litho press. Its pages were folded on a Baumfolder,
gathered by hand, bound on a Sulby Auto-Minabinda, and trimmed on a Polar
single-knife cutter.

Edited for the press by Damian Rogers
Designed by Crystal Sikma
Cover by Crystal Sikma
Cover image by RickToxik on Pixabay
Author photo by Marlowe Granados

Coach House Books
80 bpNichol Lane
Toronto ON M5S 3J4
Canada

416 979 2217
800 367 6360

mail@chbooks.com
www.chbooks.com